Universal Basic Income

UBI: An Idea Whose Time Has Come?

Philip Hugh

Legal & Disclaimer

The information contained in this book and its contents is not designed to replace nor take the place of any form of medical or professional advice; it is not meant to replace the need for independent medical, financial, legal, or other professional advice or services, as may be required. The content and information in this book have been provided for educational and entertainment purposes only.

The content and information contained in this book have been compiled from sources deemed reliable, and they are accurate to the best of the author's knowledge, information, and beliefs. However, the author cannot guarantee its accuracy and validity and cannot be held liable for any errors and/or omissions. Furthermore, changes are periodically made to this book as and when needed. Where appropriate and/or necessary, you must consult a professional (including but not limited to your doctor, attorney, financial advisor, or other professional advisors) before using any of the suggested remedies, techniques, or information in this book.

Upon using the contents and information contained in this book, you agree to hold harmless the author from and against any damages, costs, and expenses, including any legal fees potentially resulting from the application of any of the information provided by this book. This disclaimer applies to any loss, damages or injury caused by the use and application, whether directly or indirectly, of any advice or information presented, whether for breach of contract, tort, negligence, personal injury, criminal intent, or under any other cause of action.

You agree to accept all risks of using the information presented inside this book.

You agree that by continuing to read this book, where appropriate and/or necessary, you shall consult a professional (including but not limited to your doctor, attorney, or financial advisor or other advisors as needed) before using any of the suggested remedies, techniques, or information in this book. While the book refers to real-life situations, the names mentioned may have been changed.

Table of Contents

Introduction

Universal Basic Income (UBI) is not a new concept. It has been around for more than five hundred years when the idea was first introduced in a fiction socio-political satire book titled 'Utopia' by Thomas More, published in 1516. In those days, it was mainly the church and generous individuals that took care of the poor and underprivileged, which was why this book was deemed radical for its time.

In a nutshell, UBI means a guaranteed income regardless of a person's employment status. Previous famous supporters of this concept included Abraham Lincoln, Martin Luther King Jr., Thomas Jefferson, and Franklin Roosevelt. Today, this idea is supported by Bill Gates, Mark Zuckerberg, Elon Musk, and Richard Branson.

Of course, things are never straightforward, and there are as many supporters as there are critics of UBI. In this book, we will look at the concept of UBI, how it compares versus welfare, what countries that have implemented it, and the pros and cons of UBI.

Chapter 1 - What is Universal Basic Income (UBI)?

UBI, also known as citizen's basic income, basic income guarantee, or basic living stipend, is a periodic income that is paid by a Government to all individuals without any conditions. The goal of UBI is to prevent or lower the poverty rate by providing a basic income to every citizen. The characteristics of UBI are:

- Paid on an individual basis, or one payment per household.

- Automatically paid at regular intervals; weekly, or monthly, into a bank account.

- The amount, e.g., $1,000, stays the same regardless of the person's earnings go up or down.

- The amount does not vary with age. Every legal resident of the same age receives the same amount irrespective of their employment status, housing type, gender, or family structure.

- The amount is meant to cover basic needs only.

- It could be implemented locally, regionally, or nationally.

- The belief is that all citizens deserve to receive a livable income, regardless of their contribution or circumstances.

UBI - An Inevitable Result of a Robot Economy?

Currently, UBI is a hot topic because of automation and modern technology that has displaced much of the human workforce, and it is set to accelerate in the future, resulting in a "robot economy." A study by Oxford University estimated that by the year 2030, 47% of jobs in the US are at high risk of being automated. Some of the areas that are experiencing this technology revolution can already be seen in manufacturing plants that are populated wall-to-wall by robots, self-checkout lanes in supermarkets, and menus in fast-food restaurants. Right now, the technology of driverless vehicles is threatening to replace 3.5 million truck drivers in the US, and 300,000 in Canada. It is estimated that for every job lost to foreign trade, eight were lost to automation.

The common sentiments among Mark Zuckerberg, Richard Branson, and Elon Musk is that the acceleration of automation has made some countries, like the United States, very wealthy, but it has also displaced many jobs to the extent of increasing poverty rates. Therefore, there should be an alternative option before desperate people do desperate things. One alternative is that the wealth created by these new technologies should go back to the affected people via some form of UBI. Those who support this notion believe that in the long haul, UBI will cost less than the impact of poverty. Simultaneously, it might also encourage entrepreneurship and innovation among individuals who no longer have to struggle to put food on the table. On the flip side, critics fear that the implementation would be too expensive, and its unconditional nature might cause individuals to lose the desire to work.

It seems imminent that the rise of automation means more jobs will be lost. Proponents of UBI say it makes no sense for politicians to promise more 'job creations' for the people at the expense of productivity when technology can do things more efficiently. We cannot turn back the clock. More importantly, is there an effective countermeasure in place before automation forces millions of jobs to vanish, thus causing the economy to fall into recession because people no longer have the means to buy necessities?

Chapter 2 - What is the Cost of Universal Basic Income?

For those who are progressive in thinking, UBI seems like an ideal solution to counter the rise of automation. After all, a price has to be paid for lowering the poverty level and preventing an economic recession. But how much would it cost?

According to studies, an income of $1,000 per month to every American above the age of eighteen will cost taxpayers $2.4 trillion annually. This amount equals one-eighth of the country's annual economic production, and almost three-quarters of the tax revenue collected by the federal government. Opponents of UBI maintain that since it comes primarily from taxes, the people will pay significantly higher taxes, which in turn impedes the country's economic growth.

How will it be funded?

We already know that implementing UBI will not be cheap. It is a good concept, but the bottom line is who will be funding it? Perhaps a better concept is not to consider a single source but multiple sources:

- Consolidated welfare and social programs currently cost the US $1 trillion annually, if welfare programs by State and Local governments are included. Some beneficiaries will opt-in and forgo their current benefits if they choose UBI; this is estimated to save $500 Billion.

- Impose a 10% Value Added Tax (VAT) on the production of goods and services, making it impossible for large companies to hide their profits and income. Europe imposed a 20% VAT, while 160 out of 193 countries have also implemented VAT. A VAT at half of the European level could generate $800 billion in revenue. The VAT will also make more practical sense in the future since the government cannot collect income tax from robots and software.

- Currently, the US is spending $1 trillion on healthcare, homeless services, and incarceration. UBI could potentially save the country $500 billion because people can then take better care of themselves, avoiding jail, the hospital, and the street. A Prison Administrator said that people should be paid to stay out of jail because it cost so much more to jail them. Studies have shown that for every $1 given, $7 is saved in cost reductions and economic growth. For example, in terms of cost reductions, UBI given to a poor person could keep him out of jail for doing poverty induced crimes, potentially saving the government money. According to the Vera Institute of Justice, the average cost annually per inmate is $33,274, and in some states like New York, it could be as much as $69,355. In 2015, the total state expenditure on prisons across the forty-five states was a whopping $43 billion. Also, an ex-convict is less likely to re-commit, because in jail, he will not get UBI. When released from jail, his family will welcome him back because he will bring along with him his UBI.

- Giving money to the Americans has the potential to stimulate the economy by approximately $2.5 trillion and create 4.6 million new jobs, as projected by a study done by the Roosevelt Institute. The economic growth could potentially generate $800-900 billion in new revenue; this is because UBI increases entrepreneurship since people now have a safety net to venture into a business while consumers have more disposable income to purchase.

- The math above shows how approximately $2.6 trillion can be generated for UBI, and without printing new money.

Won't it Cause Massive Inflation?

People who think that UBI will cause inflation generally have the misconception that since everyone now has extra money, it means that the prices of things will increase. However, this is not necessarily the case because:

- The math, as calculated above, shows that the UBI money would only come from what is existing in the current economy. The government would not be printing new notes, which might cause existing monies to devalue. The truth is that paying more for something will not cause overall inflation because you will have less money to pay for something else, which would then cause its price to fall. Inflation is the devaluation of money generated by the printing of new notes.

- Basic commodities such as housing and rent are unlikely to increase because there is a surplus of five times more vacant houses than homeless people in the US. UBI would likely give people the means to afford a roof over their heads; rentals might decrease to stay competitive because more people can now have the freedom to move to the lowest rentals. UBI would bring businesses back to rural communities where less expensive housing is available.

- Automation and Artificial Intelligence are extremely productive, producing goods at a fraction of the cost of hiring workers. Prices of electronic products, TVs, smartphones, toys, toasters, ovens, etc., are not increasing in price, and are sometimes better. About 1.5 billion mobile phones were produced in 2019, and rising at a rate of 4.5% annually. Soon there will be more phones than people, and it will be the same for most household products. Highly automated factories will need UBI for their products to be purchased.

  Food prices will not go up because AI software will smoothen out the kinks in the supply chain, delivering farm produce more efficiently and cutting down wastage. It is estimated that 30% of food is currently wasted on their way to the market; AI will reduce that.

In a nutshell, UBI is not 'extra' free money for people to spend, which means it is unlikely to cause any significant inflationary issues.

Chapter 3 - Is Universal Basic Income better than Welfare?

The Difference between UBI and Welfare

The main difference is, UBI has no strings attached compared to welfare programs. It does not control the actions of people below the poverty line by stipulating how they should spend the money. UBI, also does not stop paying if an individual refuses to get a job, switch from full-time to part-time, gets better from a disability, or changes in their economic status. This is not a bad thing – it gives freedom of choice.

Currently, the US has many different welfare programs, mostly targeted at ensuring the poor have food and housing. All these programs require strict testing, and applicants must submit to an investigation into their needs and resources. Successful applicants often live in fear of their benefits being taken away when, for instance, they get a part-time job, or do volunteer work, or other useful activities like taking classes. UBI is more efficient at reducing poverty over the long run by giving people the chance to invest in themselves either through education or entrepreneurship. UBI is unconditional because it wants to ensure people that they do not have to worry about their day-to-day existence, or if their welfare program might fall through. It will definitely reduce stress.

UBI versus Welfare

UBI's ideal is to end poverty and revolutionize work. However, one possible disadvantage compared to welfare is that if people are not told what to do with the money, they might not spend it prudently. The other major concerns regarding UBI are:

- Fewer people will seek employment actively shrinking labor force, and therefore, lowering the economic output.

- UBI is very expensive, $1000 per adult, monthly will cost $2.4 trillion; nearly as large as the total US safety net.

- Increase in high school dropouts.

- Increased children born out of wedlock.

- Increased alcohol consumption, or buying lottery tickets.

On the other hand, welfare is not perfect either because of its drawbacks:

- Only a selected group of people qualify for welfare, so there is a stigma attached.

- Too many guidelines must be followed to remain on the program. For example, recipients need to prove their income is below the poverty line to qualify, or they must find a job within two years. Many possible recipients find it beyond their capability to fill out the application forms and have to employ lawyers. Many then give up applying for help.

- It attempts to control the behavior of the poor people who have no resources to fight back.

- Susceptible to fraud and people who cheat the system, requiring the government to employ an expensive investigation group to prevent this.

- Tends to make people dependent on handouts, and less motivated to work.

- Some recipients prolong their unemployment to the extent of becoming less employable because they let their skills and knowledge deteriorate.

- Some recipients are discouraged from getting married because their combined incomes would make them ineligible for the benefits.

- Some fathers are incentivized to live apart from their families so that their children can receive welfare.

- In 2018, there was a national increase in welfare spending amounting to $13 billion, and yet it did very little to reduce poverty.

- Another problem is that people who need welfare, cannot meet any of the guidelines, which are sometimes unfair, thus falling through the cracks.

- Welfare programs typically require people to be hitting rock bottom by being unemployed, or having zero assets to qualify. The most significant advantage of UBI is if implemented successfully, can prevent people from reaching rock bottom in the first place.

Chapter 4 – Case Studies of Universal Basic Income in Other Countries

Case Study A: Finland

In 2017, Finland was the first European country to spend $22.7 million to run a UBI experiment to assess how people would respond to the changing nature of work, and how to get people back into the workforce. Finland's Social Insurance Institution (Kela) chose 2,000 random people from across the country, who were receiving unemployment benefits between the ages of twenty-five to fifty-eight, to be replaced by UBI at €560 per month (US$637). This test was run in conjunction with a controlled group of 5,000 unemployed people under welfare.

The preliminary result after the two-year trial was:

- It made no significant changes to both groups with regard to employment.

- The most obvious benefits for the 2,000 participants came in terms of wellbeing and health, with 55% saying their health had improved and were less stressed about their financial future.

- Those on UBI discovered a new trust in the government and each other while feeling better at their prospects.

- One of the participants shared that she was motivated to take a low paying telemarketing job since her income was being supplemented by UBI, thus improving her quality of life. But after the trial ended, she had to look for a better paying job because her income decreased by €560.

- At the end of the trial period, some of the 2,000 participants were disappointed that the trial was not extended.

In conclusion, the experiment was declared neither success nor a failure. It has positively changed the participants psychologically, but it didn't help to get people into the workforce. However, the premise of this experiment is somewhat disputed because the UBI was given to unemployed recipients, and expected them to look for work. The Finland government has no immediate plans for more UBI schemes, although some hope it would be back on the table.

Case Study B: Canada

From 1974 to 1978, Canada conducted a social experiment called The Mincome Experiment in Dauphin, which was considered a low-income town as the residents fell within an income ceiling of $9,000 per family. US$2,880 was given annually to each member of 586 families for three years. The purpose of this experiment was to find out:

- The impact of UBI on both the community and the individual.

- To evaluate Canada's economic situation, identify logistic challenges, and study the ramifications of UBI.

- Whether or not UBI could replace welfare programs to eradicate poverty in the country.

- Assess the economic and social consequences of a UBI system based on the concept of negative income tax.

- What would happen to the labor supply if the country implemented UBI?

The experiment was stopped abruptly after three years because the 1970s were plagued by unusually high inflation. The conclusion of this experiment showed:

- Working hours decreased 3% for married women, 5% for unmarried women, and 1% for men.
- Decline in hospitalization
- Improved health outcomes and social wellbeing

Overall, researchers and economists of the experiment did not find the experiment particularly useful in their analysis of UBI. There was also the question of the affordability of UBI, which was deemed too high by the Canadian federal government.

Case Study C: Namibia

From 2008 to 2016, Namibia launched a UBI project called Basic Income Guarantee (BIG). The funding for BIG came from national sponsors with zero contribution from the government, which did not support the concept of UBI. The purpose of BIG was to convince the federal government of the benefits of UBI on a social level.

1,200 residents living in Otjivero, which was considered a low-income rural area, were given approximately USD$7 per month. But after two years the amount was reduced to US$5. Those over the age of sixty-years did not receive UBI because they were receiving state pensions. In 2016, BIG was stopped because the federal government officially rejected the idea of UBI in favor of stimulating economic growth.

Conclusion of BIG:

- The malnutrition rate for children under the age of five decreased by 42%.

- Local health clinics reported a five times increase in revenue because patients could now afford the treatment drugs for HIV/AIDS.

- An increase in school enrollments as families now had financial means.

- Significant decrease in crimes, e.g., poaching, petty theft, and trespassing.

- Significant decrease in household poverty.

- Increased productivity as UBI enabled people to increase their income by starting their own businesses, thus showing that free money does not necessarily cause laziness and dependency.

Case Study D: India

In 2011, India launched the "Madhya Pradesh Unconditional Cash Transfers Project" (MPUCT) in collaboration with UNICEF. The objective was to reduce poverty and economy discrepancies. Over eighteen months, 6,000 people in rural Madhya Pradesh received US$4.47 for an adult and US$2.23 for a child monthly.

Conclusion of MPUCT compared to non-UBI villages:

- A higher number of children age 14 to 18 enrolled in schools at 76% versus 51.3% in non-UBI villages.

- Increase in earnings by 21% versus 9% in non-UBI villages.

- Increase in productivity; families used the money to buy seeds, livestock, and sewing machines.

Case Study E: Alaska

In 1976, the Alaska government created the "Alaska Permanent Fund" (APF) following a black gold (oil) rush, which generated $900 million revenue to be set aside as revenues for its residents. From 1982 onwards, an annual dividend was paid to every man, woman, and child. In 2014, each Alaskan citizen (640,000) who physically resided in Alaska before the 1st January received UBI of $1,884 annually from their share of the $6.8 billion net income of the APF. The following year 2015, each resident received a UBI of $2,072 because of increased oil prices. In 2017, UBI decreased to $1,100 per person when oil prices dropped. The Alaska government is currently dealing with budget deficits; therefore UBI will be further reduced.

Findings in 2018 showed:

- UBI did not result in lesser working residents or significant changes in the employment rate.

- There was a significant increase in part-time work after implementing UBI.

- No evidence suggested that UBI had adverse economic effects on residents.

Case Study F: Kenya

The largest UBI experiment in history was launched in Kenya in 2017 by GiveDirectly, a non-profit organization.

- 6,000 people from forty villages received US$22.50 per month with no strings attached for twelve years.

- Eighty different villages received US$22.50 per month for twelve years.

- Another eighty different villages received a lump sum equivalent to two years' of UBI.

- A control group of one hundred villages received no money.

- Altogether, four groups of villages, comprising 14,474 households, were involved.

Objectives of the experiment:

- A study to produce the most comprehensive data about what happens when you give people free money.

- To answer common questions like, "Will people become lazy and stop working?" "Would they become entrepreneurs?" and "Would the money be spent on vices, e.g., alcohol and drugs, or education and skills?"

- Collect and produce comprehensive data to determine whether having financial security helps to lower poverty induced crimes, e.g., theft and violence.

- Compare the effects of giving short-term, long-term, and lump-sum payments to recipients.

- Measure outcomes of; economic status, e.g., income, assets, and consumption; time usage, e.g., work, education, risk-tasking, e.g., start-up businesses and gender relations like female empowerment.

The results after distributing $10 million showed:

- The free money also benefited neighboring villages businesses indirectly because of recipients' increased spending.

- A study estimated that every $1 invested increased the economy by $2.60

- Improved the lives of recipients, e.g., reduced hunger, increased farming and small businesses, increased assets of livestock, and iron roofs instead of mud roofs.

- Overall the regional economic expansion benefited both recipients and non-recipients of UBI.

The experiment is still ongoing at this point in writing, with more research and results forthcoming to show the magnitude of UBI on people's lives. So far, it has been very encouraging.

Case Study G: Stockton, California

In February 2019, 125 random families who lived at or below the median income of $46,000 in Stockton were selected to receive UBI of $500 per month for eighteen months. Stockton was declared bankrupt in 2012 and has an unemployment rate of 7.5% compared to the state average of 4.3%. It is also ranked 18th for child poverty among all the cities in the US.

The project's first $1 million was funded by the Economic Security Project, a non-profit organization that also sponsored funding or research for UBI projects in Oakland, Kenya, and Alaska. Michael Tubbs, the Mayor who initiated this project, wanted to show what people would do with their increased economic opportunity, e.g., re-skill, education, or new business.

Preliminary results after five months showed:

- Recipients' lives were improved.

- Recipients spent 38% on food, 24% on clothes and home supplies, 11% on utilities, 9% on gas, and 18% on miscellaneous.

- Debunk the myth that people who are struggling will use their free money on vices like alcohol, drugs, or gambling; they were using it for necessities.

- It proves that people did not become poor because they are bad at self-control and irrational decision-making, but rather it was poverty that caused them to make bad choices.

This project is still ongoing at this time of writing, and the verdict is not out yet as to whether this investment would pay off in the long run. The results so far are very positive.

Chapter 5 - Is Universal Basic Income the Way for America?

On 26 October 2019, thirty cities around the world came together to march for UBI. In the US, this march took place in New York City, Chicago, San Francisco, Salt Lake City, Orlando, and Honolulu. Some of the other countries which took part were Germany, the Netherlands, Canada, and Ghana.

The idea of UBI is currently gaining attention in the US with:

- UBI testing in Stockton and Oakland.

- Organizations like 'Income Movement,' which is testing its UBI program by giving $1,000 per month to fifty individuals across the US.

- Andrew Yang, a 2020 democratic presidential candidate signature campaign proposal is implementing 'Freedom Dividend,' UBI of $1,000 to every American adult. The purpose of Freedom Dividend is to help all Americans pay their utilities, relocate for work, stay healthy, and spend more quality time with or take care of their loved ones.

What advocators of UBI say:

- Billionaire supporters such as Richard Branson, Elon Musk, and Mark Zuckerberg, advocate implementing UBI to counter the rise in robots and AI blasting away the market for jobs.

- Tech titan Elon Musk commented that eventually, the job losses would be so severe that the government will be forced to pay people to live. There is a good chance that people will end up with UBI unless a better way is sought.

- Richard Branson, who spoke at the Nordic Business Forum 2017, said that all the new exciting innovations created will generate a lot of wealth but also reduce the number of jobs, making the idea of UBI more critical in the future as a way for the government to ensure everyone has a safety net.

- Mark Zuckerberg, in his speech at a 2017 Harvard commencement ceremony, said that giving everyone UBI is like a "cushion to try new things," and $1,000 a month for a family of five to six can be especially meaningful. He also said he could not have founded Facebook if he had to worry about getting his next meal. He also commented that Alaska's state-run cash handout program provided useful lessons for the rest of the US.

- Steward Butterfield, co-founder of Slack, tweeted his support for UBI by saying that the amount doesn't have to be much to give people a small safety net that could potentially unlock a magnitude of entrepreneurialism.

- Sam Altman, president of Silicon Valley startup 'Y Combinator,' which is also conducting a UBI test in Oakland, firmly believes that poverty takes a toll on people emotionally, and physically to the detriment of wasting their full potential. To him, UBI has the potential to undo all that.

- Andrew Yang announced that his campaign would randomly give ten American families $1,000 'Freedom Dividends' monthly for one year. There were half a million applicants by the time the contest closed on 19 September 2019. While some might see this as a gimmick, Yang's vision is to help Americans who are affected by automation by encouraging entrepreneurship and reducing poverty.

According to Schwab's 2019 Modern Wealth report, three out of five Americans are living from paycheck to paycheck, which means incomes are not keeping up with the rising daily costs of living. Half of working adults could not afford an unexpected $500 bill. Right now, UBI is having its moment in the limelight thanks to campaigns like Andrew Yang's, and billionaire entrepreneurs advocating UBI openly. The question is, would UBI open a new chapter in America?

The American Dream

The original American Dream is a belief that anyone, regardless of where or what status they were born into, can achieve their version of success through hard work, determination, and sacrifice. Today for many millennials, the American dream is more likely to be redefined as making more money than your parents. According to the latest study by Harvard University, Stanford University, and the University of California-Berkeley, only 50% of people born in the 1980s are earning more than their parents in comparison to 90% of people born in 1940s, and the numbers are getting worse. If you were born in the 2000s, your chances of doing better than your parents are about 20%. The study concluded the reasons being:

- Income inequality is the primary reason why millennials are falling behind. Currently, the top 1% of income earners capture 40-58% of all income growth as compared to 1940-1970s, whereby the top 1% captured only 4.9% of all income growth.

- The winner-take-all economic growth is leading to uneven income distribution.

- The decline of high-paying manufacturing jobs in the industrial mid-west states.

- Average earnings are suitable for the college-educated working in the right industries and in the right locations. But for those with lower skills, their average earnings are even lower now than it was fifty years ago, after considering inflation.

- Compared to earlier generations, millennials have more outstanding loans, as much as 50% more than Gen X.

The founding fathers' vision for the original American Dream is for all people to have equal and an unalienable right to opportunities, life, freedom, and the pursuit of their happiness. Is the American dream still achievable today for most people? More importantly, could UBI be the answer?

Arguments Against and For UBI

1. **AGAINST:** UBI will merely be another type of welfare to replace all welfares, but it will be more costly because it is given to everyone without conditions. Therefore, drastically inflicting

huge expenses when compared to current welfare programs, which are more focused on the conditions necessary for welfare.

FOR: However, the requirement for welfare means, testing, and investigations necessitate a huge and costly bureaucracy wasting precious money. Welfare recipients are often under constant stress to behave within the guidelines, which are not always fair. UBI reduces bureaucracy and costs of administrations since there is no need to determine who is eligible. It will not discourage people from seeking additional income for fear of losing their benefits.

2. **AGAINST:** Apprehensions about UBI replacing welfare benefits or social security because recipients' benefits might decrease under UBI.

   FOR: UBI should be designed not to eliminate, but to add to social security. It will replace most welfare benefits but on an opt-in basis. If a recipient's welfare benefit is more than UBI, they can choose not to opt-in. However, it is estimated that more than half of all of the welfare recipients will opt-in because of the freedom UBI would bring to their lives.

3. **AGAINST:** It might cause greater inequality and poverty, because UBI will be taking away welfare funds meant for housing, disability or unemployment, and will be distributing it to others who don't need the money or are already well-to-do.

   FOR: Proponents of UBI would say it will help to bridge the middle-class income gap as the majority of the wealth is going to the top 1%, while the working class remains stagnant. A $1000 per month UBI would be the same as a salary increase for everyone. This is much better than raising the minimum wage because it does not harm small businesses that cannot afford salary increases for their staff. Raising the minimum wage has, in all cases, reduced employment either by letting go of workers or closing down.

4. **AGAINST:** If the entire source of funding comes from the government, it is going to be a considerable strain and risk plunging the country into debt.

   FOR: America is the wealthiest country in the world, with an economy of over $19 trillion. The calculations in Chapter 2 show the viability of UBI without printing new money; this is the crux of the matter; if it is affordable, it should be tried.

5. **AGAINST:** Concerns about inflation because of higher demand for goods and services, but this is not necessarily true, as discussed earlier in Chapter 2.

6. **AGAINST:** Free money might de-incentivize people to work. It is better to retrain displaced workers for new jobs.

   FOR: The UBI experiment in Finland found little impact on recipients' tendency to work or not to work. However, it started on the wrong foot by giving to unemployed people and expected them to find work. It neglected the fact that most households in poverty have at least one person working and usually stuck in low paying jobs. A UBI of $1000 a month for every adult would have lifted them out of poverty. By and large retraining programs were not effective, because people are not totally malleable. For instance, it would be ludicrous to teach a coal miner or truck driver to work as a software coder.

7. **AGAINST:** Weaken social cohesion if more people choose not to work, and become isolated from colleagues, friends, and networks.

   FOR: The opposite could be the case; in America, the poverty line is $1, 200 per month. So a UBI of $1000 a month is not designed to promote laziness. It guarantees freedom of choice, and for most recipients, it will help them climb out of poverty.

UBI: An Idea whose Time has Come?

- According to a report by McKinsey & Company, by the year 2055, half of the world's work activities could be automated. In the US, 51% of jobs are susceptible to automation, and this accounts for approximately $2.7 trillion in wages. The most affected jobs are in manufacturing, food services, retail, and truck driving. Experts have predicted that one out of three Americans' jobs will be replaced by technology in the next twelve years. Ultimately, millions of lives will be in upheaval as jobs disappear.

- There is this argument that automation is not new, and that previous industrial revolutions led by machines have not caused any job losses. Indeed, more jobs were created. There was the first industrial revolution in the 18th century, the second in the early 20th century, and the third industrial revolution in the second half of the 20th century culminating in the rise of electronics. More jobs were created than were lost, until now. We are in the midst of the fourth industrial revolution led by robots and artificial intelligence. Massive factories are being populated wall-to-wall by robots. Self-service counters have replaced people. Within five years, 30% of the malls and main street shops will be closed by eCommerce. Three million call center workers will be replaced by AI software. Within ten to twenty years, three million truck drivers will be replaced by robot trucks that never stop. Seven million jobs at truck stops in danger of disappearing. The rise of robots and AI will accelerate, so will job losses. UBI may be inevitable.

- Work is being executed more efficiently by robots, AI, and software. There is nothing wrong with that if displaced workers are given a slice of the economic gains. Robots should not only take away work but also work for the people. Advocates of UBI argue that a robot economy should be regarded as a national resource; after all, such an economy cannot exist without people.

- Based on a UBI of $1,000 per month to Americans aged between eighteen and sixty-four, starting in 2021, the Roosevelt Institute estimated it could increase the economy by 12-13%, or the equivalent of $2.5 trillion by 2025. With more disposable income, a town of 5,000 people, each annually receiving $12,000 could inject an additional $60 million into the local community. Imagine this scenario being multiplied throughout parts of America.

- UBI encourages recipients to find work, unlike many welfare programs that take away benefits when recipients find work.

- Reduces bureaucracy and cost of administrations since there is no need to determine who is eligible. This is very significant because many possible welfare recipients are unable to fill a whole stack of bewildering forms required to qualify.

- It helps to bridge the middle-class income gap as the majority of the wealth are going to the top 1%, while the working class remains stagnant.

- Encourages entrepreneurship by giving people a safety net if their business fails. The Roosevelt Institute estimated 4.6 million job creations and a 12% economic growth. It is near impossible to start a business with zero capital.

- Gives workers who are working in exploitative wages and abusive conditions the leverage to seek better terms or employment.

- Improves labor market efficiency and increases national productivity because people are no longer forced to take jobs they dislike or are a bad fit, making them unmotivated at their jobs. They can now seek positive career growth by finding work that is more compatible and fulfilling, thus becoming more productive. Having money is very empowering.

- Improves mental health of recipients by reducing major stressors, e.g., poverty, scarcity, and financial insecurity.

- Improves physical health as increased financial security makes people less prone to stresses, disease, or self-destructive behavior - for example, reduction in hospitalization rates and visits to the emergency rooms due to domestic violence.

- Reduces domestic violence, suicides, reduces crime, and gun violence.

- Improves relationships by reducing conflicts caused by financial stress or giving victims of domestic violence or child abuse the mobility to get out of the abusive relationship.

- It promotes smarter decision-making in recipients. Research has shown that poverty and financial insecurity reduces one's decision-making ability by thirteen IQ points. UBI would give people the security they need so that they can focus on more meaningful things.

- Recognizes the work done by millions of stay-at-home mothers and caregivers who are doing some of the most important work in daily lives, and yet the market values their work at zero.

- Around the world, UBI has proven to be the most effective way to reduce poverty. In 2015, Alaska was ranked second best in the US for income inequality, and this was credited mainly to their implementation of UBI. Before UBI, they were ranked 18th.

- Contrary to concerns that recipients would use their free money on vices or stop working, World Bank has shown that such behaviors are reduced. (Read the full report here http://blogs.worldbank.org/impactevaluations/do-poor-waste-transfers-booze-and-cigarettes-no). Another good example right under our noses is the Alaska Permanent Fund, of which the people regularly spend their dividends on their children's education, which dispels the stereotype of poor people being irresponsible with their money.

How Will UBI Change People's Lives?

- Some people will use UBI as their primary source of income, while others will treat this as a supplement to their existing income. Overall, UBI shouldn't have a negative impact on people's motivation to work because the amount given won't be enough to tempt them to quit their jobs, and those already established in their careers are unlikely to quit the corporate ladder for $1,000. The more likelihood is that people will have the freedom to resign from jobs they are unsatisfied with and look for more suitable ones or switch to part-time jobs, start their own business, or choose to stay at home to look after their young children or the elderly. UBI will give people more choices and flexibility in their work lives. For example, a security guard at a mall who has been laid off by robotic mall cops can use his UBI as a buffer while he looks for another job or re-trains, but it won't be enough for him to stay out of the workforce for good.

- It helps to support, and improve the lives of women who do not have equal employment opportunities as men. In some cases, it also reduces the dependency of women on men for their survival, especially if they are trapped in an abusive relationship. Furthermore, when a woman has children, the main responsibility of raising the children often falls on them. With UBI, some women can choose not to work to support their children, and instead, focus on raising them.

- Unpaid care workers who have to quit their jobs to look after their young children, elderly, ill or disabled relatives can support themselves while making a social contribution. It also takes the pressure off social services that provide healthcare to the sick and elderly.

- One common concern is that people will use their UBI on vices like drinking, gambling, or drugs. On the contrary, UBI might make it easier for people to 'pressure' their neighbors into good behavior. For example, a person who is irresponsible and spent all his money drinking tries to plead helplessness and borrows from his friends and relatives. Since they know he receives the same UBI of $1,000, they are more likely to pressure him to clean up his act and deal with his issues; no more excuses. Imagine such social intervention multiplied throughout the country, and it will probably be much more effective than the existing help from social services or bureaucracies.

- UBI gives people the foundation to be more responsible for their lives. It is hard for poor people to be responsible, plan, and think about the future when they are busy trying to make ends meet and put food on the table. A feeling of scarcity often leads to wrong results.

- Contrary to mainstream beliefs, it is not jobs that lead to money, but money that creates money. E.g., in the board game, Monopoly, everyone starts with a bit of money. One cannot play the game starting with zero money; real life is the same. Without money, one cannot pay for transport, food, clothes, or education, all of which are used to fuel a thriving economy.

- More unemployed people will seek part-time, freelance, creative, or project-based work, work they find satisfying but low paying. Alternatively, UBI gives them the incentives to seek better opportunities. This is much better than welfare, which tends to hold them back from accepting small assignments or jobs because of the fear of losing their unemployment benefits. It is all about having more freedom.

- People's quality of life will improve because their fundamental needs are met, even if their circumstances change substantially, e.g., their business is struggling, or long-term illness. They have UBI to fall back on and help them through difficult times, and this surely must be the situation in our modern times that hopefully leads to a Star Trek future?

- People will be more willing to take risks and start a business. Even though there will be some failures, risk-taking is the way to progress toward new breakthroughs, products, and services.

- Encourages the creative potential of people such as inventors, designers, artists, and musicians who often need time to develop their talents and potential. That was how Facebook was founded. Mark Zuckerberg said that it was only possible because he did not have to worry about his next meal.

- Promotes work-life balance, and more freedom to cut back on working hours if people need to spend more time with their family, e.g., taking care of a new baby.

In the 1960s, Dr. Martin Luther King Jr., who supported the idea of a 'guaranteed income,' said people would thrive and have the means to seek self-improvement when they have the guarantee that their income is stable and absolute. Famous economist Milton Friedman and more than a thousand economists supported the idea of UBI. During the Nixon Administration, a form of UBI called the 'Family Assistance Plan' passed the House of Representatives twice before failing at the Senate. Ironically, it failed because some in the Senate thought it did not go far enough; they regretted that years later.

Ultimately, the only way to find out if UBI works for America is to implement it through careful planning. In the meantime, rising income inequality, stagnant wages, and AI taking over people's jobs is accelerating at an increasing rate, which means the American government needs to address this sooner rather than later. The big question is, what will happen if America continues to wait and see while more people are falling behind?

When farms were being mechanized and machines started appearing in factories in the early 20th century, thousands of jobs were lost. There were widespread riots, destruction of properties, and loss of lives. In this fourth industrial revolution, not thousands but millions of jobs will disappear. The upheaval could well be ten times greater.

Wouldn't it be wiser to bite the bullet now by implementing UBI, rather than to wait till the point of extreme inequality, and mass income loss has come to pass? Either way, it is a decision that must be made.

Chapter 6 - Debunking Myths about Universal Basic Income

There is no doubt of many uncertainties concerning UBI. However, some of the concerns tend to focus on myths and ignorance due to a lack of proper understanding of how UBI works. This confusion and misinformation can cause the average person to be unreceptive even before they give the idea of UBI a fair chance.

Free money will make people less motivated to work

The answer is no, as can be seen from various UBI experiments discussed in earlier chapters especially, compared to welfare programs. This is because welfare benefits get reduced or lost if recipients find work. They are no better off financially if they work harder, so why bother receiving welfare? Ironically, the welfare system keeps the beneficiary in a poverty cycle instead of encouraging them to move out of their comfort zone. With UBI, people will be more willing to step up because they don't have the fear of losing their benefits (see Chapter 4). As explained, the amount given is not going to make anyone rich enough to give up their jobs. By the way, people who said there should be no free money are often receiving free money themselves, like sons of billionaires, and many politicians.

Isn't UBI a form of Communism?

Essentially the answer is no. UBI is a policy, while Communism is a political and economic system. In Communism, all resources are owned by the state, and the wealth is divided among citizens. Whereas, UBI does not remove private ownership of capital, and people will continue to pay taxes, own their homes, businesses, and vehicles, etc. UBI does not do away with people's free choice, private capital, or property, and it means more freedom for people to fulfill their dreams and desires.

Is it unfair for UBI to be giving away 'your money' to other people?

Consider the tax money that is being used to fund public schools, public transport, and public healthcare. Should a person who pays less or zero tax be allowed to use roads that were built with tax money? The police and fire departments are run with tax money, and yet they provide equal protection to everyone, regardless of how much tax they pay. If you pay tax, then you will also get a chunk of it back through UBI. Perhaps a more appropriate question would be, "Is paying for UBI a good use of tax money, even though it can potentially benefit a lot of people in the society? What are the costs versus benefits?" The calculations given in Chapter 2 show that America can afford UBI of $1000 per month for every citizen, eighteen years and above. If that is the case, it would be unconscionable not to have UBI.

Also, it surely is right to consider that citizens are shareholders and owners of the country. America would not be the wealthiest country in the world without its citizens.

UBI will invite an influx of immigrants

Some concerns implementing UBI is that it will lead to an influx of immigrants looking for a free, stable income. However, UBI will only be paid to citizens of the country. Migrants may be more welcomed since they will be paying taxes, thereby contributing to UBI, so there are no immediate incentives for emigration merely for the sake of UBI.

Why would you give UBI to rich people like Bill Gates?

Universal Basic Income is universal, and for every citizen, and because it is universal, there is no stigma attached to it, unlike welfare programs. It can have a unifying effect for a country because if you get UBI, you must be a citizen - "you get it, and I get it." Why not the rich, after all, they pay more in taxes, or in Value Added Tax (VAT); much more than they receive in UBI. Citizens would not mind the millionaires and wealthy corporations so much because they will be paying more VAT.

Dr. Karl Widerquist, an American economist and associate professor, explains that UBI is a negative tax because what you pay the government is a positive tax, but what the government pays you (UBI) is a negative tax. For the rich, their positive tax is higher than the negative tax, whereas it is vice-versa for the poor.

Conclusion

Thank you for reading this book and for investing time in educating yourself about Universal Basic Income.

Like most financial concepts, UBI has its unique pros and cons. Although UBI will not solve all our problems, it does offer a fresh approach to the current welfare policy, and undoubtedly will financially benefit some people more than others.

Lastly, now that you know enough about UBI, perhaps you can start by forming your opinion, and consider how it will affect you if the government is to implement it later down the road.

Yours truly,

Philip Hugh